MAKING DISCIPLES FOR CHRIST IN SEVEN DAYS

PASTOR OTHNEL PIERRE

World rights reserved. This book or any portion thereof may not be copied or reproduced in any form or manner whatever, except as provided by law, without the written permission of the publisher, except by a reviewer who may quote brief passages in a review.

The author assumes full responsibility for the accuracy of all facts and quotations as cited in this book. The opinions expressed in this book are the author's personal views and interpretations, and do not necessarily reflect those of the publisher.

This book is provided with the understanding that the publisher is not engaged in giving spiritual, legal, medical, or other professional advice. If authoritative advice is needed, the reader should seek the counsel of a competent professional.

Copyright © 2021 Pastor Othnel Pierre
Copyright © 2021 TEACH Services, Inc.
ISBN-13: 978-1-4796-1317-5 (Paperback)
ISBN-13: 978-1-4796-1318-2 (ePub)
Library of Congress Control Number: 2021911016

All Bible references are taken from the King James Version of the Bible. Public domain.

DEDICATION

This collection of messages is dedicated to my 86-year-old father, Pastor Anélus Pierre, who selflessly initiated me into the art of loving the work of God and the Adventist Movement.

To Édithe Pierre, my wife, friend, confidant, and mother of my three children: Anne-France, Laur Douny Edine, and Auguste, who suffered with me and supported me during the preparation of this booklet.

To my brothers, Josué, Etzer, Bossuet, Mirtyl, Sandy, and my only sister, Carline, all of them devotedly serving the Master. Glory be to his name.

To Sister Cléramise Alexis, baptized member of Morija Seventh-day Adventist Church, Manhattan, NY, with whom I share the same birthday. She encouraged me, even commanded me, to gather my sermons and messages in a collection. This is a foretaste of that. Keep praying for me Sister Alexis!

TABLE OF CONTENTS

Dedication . . . . *iii*
Introduction 7
Foreword #1. 11
Foreword #2 25

SIMPLE AND ESSENTIAL TRUTHS #1

BY PASTOR OTHNEL PIERRE—2020

FAITH. 27

SIMPLE AND ESSENTIAL TRUTHS #2

BY PASTOR OTHNEL PIERRE—2020

THE BIBLE 30

SIMPLE AND ESSENTIAL TRUTHS #3

BY PASTOR OTHNEL PIERRE—2020

THE SABBATH 33

SIMPLE AND ESSENTIAL TRUTHS #4

BY PASTOR OTHNEL PIERRE—2020

THE STATE OF THE DEAD. 39

SIMPLE AND ESSENTIAL TRUTHS #5
BY PASTOR OTHNEL PIERRE—2020
HEALTH PRINCIPLES 44

SIMPLE AND ESSENTIAL TRUTHS #6
PREPARED BY PASTOR OTHNEL PIERRE—2020
THE LORD'S SUPPER 52

SIMPLE AND ESSENTIAL TRUTHS #7
PREPARED BY PASTOR OTHNEL PIERRE—2020
FIDELITY EXERCISES 58

In conclusion… 64
Reviews. 65

INTRODUCTION

"The monotony of our service for God needs to be broken up. Every church-member should be engaged in some special service for the Master. Let those who are well established in the truth go into neighboring places, and hold meetings. Let God's Word be read, and let the ideas expressed be such that they will be readily comprehended by all"—(Ellen White, *The Review and Herald*, May 5, 1904, par. 5).

Making Disciples for Christ in Seven Days is a small collection of presentations prepared by Pastor Othnel Pierre during his ministry in 2020 in the Morija District, Manhattan, NY, and Mitspa, White Plains, NY.

It was written in response to personal evangelistic concerns during the confinement of humanity at a time when the scourge of the novel coronavirus, Covid-19, was rampant in the world. However, this collection can be used at any time and under any circumstances. The spirit of adaptation and creativity of each person will determine its use.

It should be stated clearly that we can no longer rely solely on public evangelization campaigns in which a single actor, a star preacher, and a few assistant evangelists, traditionally known as "Bible readers," perform while the Church of the Lord sits in admiration, like spectators in a theater.

It is time for believers to pull themselves together and remember that each member, upon entering the church through baptism or profession of faith, becomes a missionary charged with advancing the growth of God's kingdom.

It is for this purpose that we offer you this Study Manual, called: *"Simple and Essential Truths."*

The strategy to be used is thus suggested:

The church pastor or the Director of the Personal Ministries Department or the First Elder, in consultation with the church committee, calls for volunteers for personal evangelism.

This number of volunteers shall be determined by the membership of the congregation in question, bearing in mind the baptismal goal proposed by the Conference of which that congregation is a part.

As soon as the list of volunteers is completed, a refresher course will be organized for them. Volunteers will diligently go through this short refresher session. Begin with forewords #1 and #2 then follow with the actual study series. This series will cover the presentation of seven key topics, as much as possible, over several consecutive days.

These studies will be shared by the volunteers, in turn, with two people of their choice among parents, children, companions, friends, co-workers, neighbors, etc. Each presentation will last between 15 and 30 minutes and will take place at a frequency agreed upon by the parties.

Once the volunteers have studied the seven topics (Faith, the Bible, the Sabbath, Fate of the Dead, Health Care Practices, The Lord's Supper, Faithfulness Practices) with the two people of their choice, they will guide them toward three consecutive days of decision making or decision reinforcement. This will be followed by baptism or a ceremony of reception of members through profession of faith. Isn't this wonderful?

In *Testimonies for the Church,* vol. 6, pages 305 and 306, or in *Christian Service,* page 270, we note this thought from the pen of Sister Ellen G. White: "All who surrender themselves to God in unselfish service for humanity are in cooperation with the Lord of glory. This thought sweetens all toil, it braces the will, it nerves the spirit for whatever may befall."

Let us win souls for heaven and according to the Handmaid of the Lord, let us work towards a crown encrusted with stars that we will soon lay at the feet of Jesus. Amen!

Suggested theme songs:

1. 541 (H&L) Volunteers in combat
2. 530 (H&L) Voluntary standing for big battles
3. 537 (H&L) Put on your weapons, volunteer
4. A call is coming in for soldiers

Since the other songs are in our official French Hymnes et Louanges collection, I am giving you a bonus of the 4th song translated:

1-
A call comes for soldiers.
It is for everyone.
Soldiers for the conflict,
Do you hear the call?
Will you also respond with dedication?
Have you enlisted
as a volunteer?

Refrain
Volunteers for Jesus
Real soldiers.
Others are enlisted.
Why not you?
Christ is the Captain
We will not be afraid.
Will you be enlisted as a volunteer?

2-
Yes, Jesus is calling.
Courageous solders
Soldiers who will follow

Him closely every day.
Him this brave hero
Wants to train us.
Will you be enlisted as a volunteer?

3-
Christ also calls you
to train the soldiers
Yourself, be valiant
a mighty leader
He will crown you
When he comes back
Will you be enlisted as a volunteer?

FOREWORD #1

- Types of prayer
- Knowledge of the position of the books of the Bible. Those who are interested should also have an idea of the number of chapters in each book.
- Learn how to answer Bible-related questions, about Jesus, with the aid of one or more biblical texts. (Mark 2:25; Luke 24:27)
- Let those you have chosen (both of them) for the seven key topics know that this is not all, but that they need to commit themselves to Christ and be baptized.

Types of Prayer

For Christians, praying means: "asking fervently, supplicating, or even begging." It is an invocation or an act that seeks to activate a relationship, a communion with God. We should learn to pray. Jesus taught his disciples how to pray in Luke 11:1–13.

The most common types of prayer are: invocation, intercession, and benediction.

A prayer of invocation is a request for God's spiritual presence and blessing at the beginning of a ceremony or event, in which God is asked to hear prayers of petition that are offered to Him.

A prayer of intercession is the act of praying for others or on behalf of others. A wonderful example of a prayer of intercession is found in Daniel 9. The following is only a partial list of those for whom we should offer prayers of intercession: all those in positions of authority (public and religious) (1 Tim. 2:2), ministers (Phil. 1: 19), friends (Job 42:8), countrymen (Rom. 10:1), the sick (James 5:14), enemies (Jer. 29:7), those who persecute us (Matt. 5:44), those who forsake us (2 Tim. 4:16), and everybody (1 Tim. 2:1).

A prayer of benediction is usually said 1—at the close of a worship service (Num. 6:24–27; 2 Cor. 13:14; Heb. 13:20, 21; 1 Thess. 5:23, 24; Rom. 15:33); 2—on the emblems of the Lord's Supper (Matt. 26:26–30); 3—on houses and other properties (1 Kings 8:26–28).

The Books of the Bible

Old Testament

The Old Testament is the first part of the Bible in most books of its kind. The name represents God's original promise (to Abraham's descendants in particular) before the coming of Jesus Christ in the New Testament (or the New Promise). The Old Testament covers the creation of the universe, the history of the Patriarchs, the exodus from Egypt, the rise of Israel as a nation, the subsequent decline and fall of Israel, the Prophets (who spoke in the name of God), and the Books of Wisdom.

1. **Genesis: 50 chapters.** Genesis speaks of the beginnings and is fundamental to understanding the rest of the Bible. It is ultimately a book that talks about relationships, highlighting those between God and His creation, between God and mankind, and between human beings.
2. **Exodus: 40 chapters.** Exodus describes the story of the Israelites leaving Egypt after slavery. The book establishes a fundamental theology in which God reveals His name, His attributes, His redemption, His law, and how He is to be worshipped.
3. **Leviticus: 27 chapters.** Leviticus takes its name from the Septuagint (the pre-Christian Greek translation of the Old Testament) and means "about the Levites" (the priests of Israel). It serves as a manual of regulations for the Holy King to establish His earthly throne among the people of His kingdom. This book explains how priests, Levites, and people are to behave as a holy nation and how they are to worship God in holiness.
4. **Numbers: 36 chapters.** Numbers traces the story of Israel's journey from Mount Sinai to the plains of Moab on the border of Canaan. The book records the murmuring and rebellion of God's people and their subsequent judgment.
5. **Deuteronomy: 34 chapters.** Deuteronomy ("the second statement of the Law") serves as a reminder to God's people about

> *The Old Testament is the first part of the Bible in most books of its kind. The name represents God's original promise (to Abraham's descendants in particular) before the coming of Jesus Christ in the New Testament (or the New Promise).*

His covenant. The book represents a "pause" before Joshua's conquest of the Promised Land begins. The book is also a reminder of the exigencies of serving God's will.

6. **Joshua: 24 chapters.** Joshua is a story of conquest and fulfillment by God's people. After many years of slavery in Egypt and forty years in the desert, the Israelites were finally allowed to enter the land promised to their fathers.

7. **Judges: 21 chapters.** The book of Judges depicts the life of Israel in the Promised Land from the death of Joshua to the rise of the monarchy. It recounts the urgent appeals made to God by the people in times of crisis and apostasy, which made necessary the office of Judges raised up by the Lord. Through them, the Lord brings down foreign oppressors and restores peace to the country.

8. **Ruth: 4 chapters.** Ruth's book has been called one of the best examples of a short story ever written. It presents the story of a remnant keeping true faith and piety in the time of the judges through the sinking and restoration of Naomi and her daughter-in-law Ruth (ancestor of King David and Jesus).

9. **1 Samuel: 31 chapters.** 1 Samuel tells the story of God's establishment of a political system in Israel led by a human king. Through Samuel's life we see the rise of the monarchy and the tragedy of its first king, Saul.

10. **2 Samuel: 24 chapters.** After the failure of King Saul in 1 Samuel, 2 Samuel portrays David as a true (though imperfect) representative of the ideal theocratic king. During David's reign, the Lord made the nation prosperous, defeated its enemies, and fulfilled His promises.

11. **1 Kings: 22 chapters.** 1 Kings continues the story of the monarchy in Israel and God's involvement through the prophets. After David, his son Solomon ascends the throne of a united kingdom, although this unity lasts only during his reign. The book explores how each subsequent king in Israel and Judah responds to God's call and how they often failed to do so.

12. **2 Kings: 25 chapters.** 2 Kings continues with the historical account of Judah and Israel. The kings of each nation are judged in the light of their obedience to the covenant with God. In the end, the peoples of both nations are driven into exile because of their disobedience.
13. **1 Chronicles: 22 chapters.** Just as the author of the books of Kings had structured and narrated the history of Israel to meet the needs of the exiled community, the author of 1 Chronicles wrote another story for the restored community.
14. **2 Chronicles: 36 chapters.** 2 Chronicles continues the story of Israel's history with an eye on the restoration of those who had returned from exile.
15. **Ezra: 10 chapters.** The book of Ezra tells how God's covenant people were restored from Babylonian exile to the covenant land as a theocratic community (kingdom of God), even while continuing to be under foreign rule.
16. **Nehemiah: 13 chapters.** Close to the book of Ezra, Nehemiah recounts the return of this "king's cupbearer" and the challenges he and the other Israelites face in their restored homeland.
17. **Esther: 10 chapters.** The book of Esther relates the institution of the annual Purim Festival through the historical account of Esther, a Jewish girl who becomes Queen of Persia and saves her people from destruction.
18. **Job: 42 chapters.** Through a series of monologues, the book of Job tells the story of a righteous man who suffers under terrible circumstances. The deep ideas of the book, its literary structures, and the quality of its rhetoric show the genius of the author.
19. **Psalms: 150 chapters.** The Psalms are collections of songs and poems, divided into five books, which represent centuries of praise and prayers to God on a number of themes and circumstances. The Psalms are lively, concrete, and full of emotion; they are rich in imagery, comparison, and metaphor.

20. **Proverbs: 31 chapters.** Proverbs was written to give "prudence to the simple, knowledge and discretion to the young," to make the wise even wiser. Frequent references to "my son" emphasize the instruction to the youth, guiding them to a way of life that yields rewarding results.
21. **Ecclesiastes: 12 chapters.** The author of Ecclesiastes puts his power of wisdom to work in examining human experience and assessing the situation of humanity. His point of view is limited to what is happening "under the sun" (as is the case with all human teachers).
22. **Song of Solomon: 8 chapters.** In ancient Israel, everything in the life of man passed through the expression of words: reverence, gratitude, anger, pain, suffering, trust, friendship, commitment. In the Song of Solomon we find love expressed in inspired words that reveal its exquisite charm and beauty as one of God's most excellent gifts.
23. **Isaiah: 66 chapters.** Isaiah, son of Amoz, is often considered the greatest of the prophets of the Holy Scriptures. His name means "The Lord saves." Isaiah is a book that reveals all the dimensions of God's judgment and salvation.
24. **Jeremiah: 52 chapters.** This book preserves an account of Jeremiah's prophetic ministry, whose personal life and struggles are shown to us in far greater depth and detail than those of any other Old Testament prophet.
25. **Lamentations: 5 chapters.** The Lamentations, as the name suggests, consist of a series of poetic and powerful lamentations about the destruction of Jerusalem (the royal city of the Lord's kingdom) in 586 BC.
26. **Ezekiel: 48 chapters.** The Old Testament in general and the prophets in particular presuppose and teach God's sovereignty over all creation and the course of history. Nowhere in the Bible is God's initiative and control more clearly and widely expressed than in the book of Prophet Ezekiel.

27. **Daniel: 12 chapters.** The book of Daniel summarizes the great events in the life of the prophet Daniel during the exile of Israel. His life and visions highlight God's plans for redemption and God's sovereign control of mankind.
28. **Hosea: 14 chapters.** Prophet Hosea, son of Beeri, lived in the tragic last days of the Northern Kingdom. His life served as a parable of God's faithfulness to an unfaithful people of Israel.
29. **Joel: 3 chapters.** Prophet Joel warned the people of Judah about God's coming judgment and the future restoration and blessing that will come through repentance.
30. **Amos: 9 chapters.** Amos prophesied during the reigns of Osiah over Judah (792–740 BC) and Jeroboam II over Israel (793–753).
31. **Obadiah: 1 chapter.** Prophet Obadiah warned the proud people of Edom about the impending judgment that will come upon them.
32. **Jonah: 4 chapters.** Jonah is surprising as a prophetic book in that it is a narrative account of Jonah's mission to the city of Nineveh, his resistance, his imprisonment in a large fish, his visit to the city, and the result that followed.
33. **Micah: 7 chapters.** Micah prophesied between 750 and 686 BC during the reigns of Jotham, Ahaz, and Hezekiah, kings of Judah. Israel was in a state of apostasy. Micah predicted the fall of its capital, Samaria, and also the inevitable desolation of Judah.
34. **Nahum: 3 chapters.** The book contains the "vision of Nahum," whose name means "comfort." The focal point of the whole book is the Lord's judgment on Nineveh for its oppression, cruelty, idolatry, and wickedness.
35. **Habakkuk: 3 chapters.** Very little is known about Habakkuk; he is only remembered as a contemporary of Jeremiah and a man of strong faith. The book bearing his name contains a dialogue between the prophet and God about injustice and suffering.
36. **Zephaniah: 3 chapters.** Prophet Zephaniah was obviously a person of considerable social standing in Judah and was probably of

royal lineage. The author's intention was to announce to Judah the imminence of God's judgment.

37. **Haggai: 2 chapters.** Haggai was a prophet who, together with Zechariah, encouraged the returning exiles to rebuild the temple. His prophecies clearly show the consequences of disobedience. When the people give priority to God and his temple, they are blessed.
38. **Zechariah: 14 chapters.** Like Jeremiah and Ezekiel, Zechariah was not only a prophet but also a member of a priestly family. Zechariah's (and Haggai's) main purpose was to rebuke the people of Judah, to encourage and motivate them to complete the reconstruction of the temple.
39. **Malachi: 4 chapters.** Malachi, whose name means "my messenger," addressed the Israelites after their return from exile. The theological message of the book can be summed up in one sentence: the Great King will come not only to judge His people, but also to bless and restore them.

And "Now the New Testament"

The New Testament is a collection of 27 books, usually placed after the Old Testament in most Christian Bibles. The name refers to the new covenant (or promise) between God and mankind through the death and resurrection of Jesus Christ. The New Testament records the life and ministry of Jesus, the growth and impact of the early church, and instruction to early churches.

1. **Matthew: 28 chapters.** Matthew's main purpose in writing his Gospel (the "good news") is to prove to his Jewish readers that Jesus is their Messiah. He does this primarily by showing how Jesus, through His life and ministry, fulfilled the Old Testament Scriptures.

2. **Mark: 16 chapters.** Since Mark's Gospel (the "good news") is traditionally associated with Rome, it may have been occasioned by the persecutions of the Roman church in the period around AD 64–67. Mark may have written to prepare his readers for such suffering by placing the life of our Lord before them.
3. **Luke: 24 chapters.** Luke's Gospel (the "good news") was written to strengthen the faith of all believers and to respond to the attacks of unbelievers. It was presented to demystify some of the unfounded stories reported about Jesus that had nothing to do with Him. Luke wanted to show that the place of the Gentile (non-Jewish) Christian in the kingdom of God is based on Jesus' teaching.

> *The New Testament is a collection of 27 books, usually placed after the Old Testament in most Christian Bibles. The name refers to the new covenant (or promise) between God and mankind through the death and resurrection of Jesus Christ.*

4. **John: 21 chapters.** John's Gospel (the "good news") is quite different from the other three. It highlights events that are not detailed in the others. The author himself clearly states his main purpose in 20:31: "that you may believe that Jesus is the Christ, the Son of God, and believing that you can have life in His name."
5. **Acts: 28 chapters.** The book of Acts establishes a bridge between the writings of the New Testament and the Gospels. It is presented as a second volume of the Gospel of Luke. It connects what Jesus "began to do and teach" as recorded in the Gospels with what He continued to do and teach through the preaching of the apostles and the establishment of the Church.
6. **Romans: 16 chapters.** Paul's main theme in the Epistle to the Romans is the presentation of the Gospel (the "good news"),

God's plan of salvation, and righteousness for all mankind, Jew and non-Jew.

7. **1 Corinthians: 16 chapters.** The first letter to the Corinthians revolves around the theme of problems of Christian conduct in the church. It is about progressive sanctification—the continuous development of a holy character. Obviously, Paul was personally concerned about the problems of the Corinthians, thereby demonstrating the heart of a true pastor (shepherd).
8. **2 Corinthians: 13 chapters.** Because of the occasion that prompted the writing of this letter, Paul had a number of goals in mind: to express the comfort and joy he felt because the Corinthians had responded favorably to his overwhelming letter when he told them about the problems he went through in the province of Asia, and to explain to them the true nature (the joys, sufferings, and rewards) and high calling of the Christian ministry.
9. **Galatians: 6 chapters.** Galatians stands as an eloquent and vigorous apologetic for the essential truth of the New Testament: that people are justified by faith in Jesus Christ, no more and no less, and that they are sanctified not by legalistic works, but by the obedience that comes from faith in God's work through them.
10. **Ephesians: 6 chapters.** Unlike many of Paul's other letters, the Epistle to the Ephesians does not deal with any particular error or heresy. Paul wrote to broaden his readers' horizons so that they could better understand the dimensions of God's eternal purpose and grace and come to appreciate the high purposes God has for the church.
11. **Philippians: 4 chapters.** Paul's primary purpose in writing this letter was to thank the Philippians for the gift they had sent him upon learning that he was being held in Rome. However, he takes this opportunity to touch on several other points: (1) to give an account of his own situation; (2) to encourage the Philippians to stand firm in the face of persecution and to rejoice under any circumstances; and (3) to urge them to humility and unity.

12. **Colossians: 4 chapters.** Paul's purpose is to refute the Colossian heresy. To achieve this goal, he exalts Christ as the very image of God, the Creator, the pre-existent sustainer of all things, the head of the church, the first risen one, the fullness of the divinity (God) in corporeal form, and the reconciler.
13. **1 Thessalonians: 5 chapters.** Although the orientation of the letter is varied, the subject of eschatology (doctrine of last things) seems to predominate in both letters to the Thessalonians. Each chapter of 1 Thessalonians ends with a reference to the Second Coming of Christ.
14. **2 Thessalonians: 3 chapters.** Since the situation in the Thessalonian church has changed only slightly, Paul's purpose in writing this letter is the same as in his first letter. He writes (1) to encourage persecuted believers, (2) to correct a misunderstanding concerning the return of the Lord, and (3) to urge the Thessalonians to be steadfast and to work for their daily bread.
15. **1 Timothy: 6 chapters.** On his fourth missionary journey, Paul had asked Timothy to look after the church at Ephesus while he went to Macedonia. When he realized that he might not return to Ephesus in the near future, he wrote this first letter to Timothy to elaborate in detail the mission he had entrusted to his young assistant. This is the first of the "Pastoral Epistles."
16. **2 Timothy: 4 chapters.** Paul was concerned for the welfare of the churches in this period of persecution under Nero, and he exhorted Timothy to keep the gospel, persevere in it, continue to preach it, and, if necessary, suffer for it. This is the second "Pastoral Epistle."
17. **Titus: 3 chapters.** Apparently, Paul introduced Christianity to Crete when he and Titus visited the island. Thereafter, he left Titus there to organize the converts. Paul sent out letters to Zenas and Aplos, who were traveling to a place that required them to go through Crete, to give Titus personal permission and advice on how to counter opposition, instructions on faith and conduct,

and warnings about false teachers. This is the last of the "Pastoral Epistles."

18. **Philemon: 1 chapter.** In order to obtain from Philemon the voluntary acceptance of the return of the fugitive slave Onesimus to his service, Paul writes to him with great tact and light tone, a letter in which he uses a lot of puns. His request is organized in the manner prescribed by the ancient Greek and Roman masters: establishing relationships, persuading the mind, and touching emotions.

19. **Hebrews: 13 chapters.** The theme of Hebrews is the absolute supremacy and sovereignty of Jesus Christ as the Revelator and Mediator of God's grace. A striking feature of this presentation of the gospel is the author's unique way of presenting eight specific passages from the Old Testament Scriptures.

20. **James: 5 chapters.** The characteristics present in the letter are: (1) an unquestionable Jewish background; (2) an emphasis on vital Christianity, characterized by good works and a faith that works (authentic faith must and will be accompanied by a coherent way of life); (3) its organization is simple; (4) and the author's familiarity with the teachings of Jesus, which have come to us through the Sermon on the Mount, is evident.

21. **1 Peter: 5 chapters.** Although 1 Peter is a short letter, it touches on various doctrines and has much to say about Christian life and duties. Not surprisingly, many readers have found that it has different main themes. For example, the epistle was characterized as a letter of separation, suffering and persecution, suffering and glory, hope, pilgrimage, courage, and as a letter dealing with the true grace of God.

22. **2 Peter: 3 chapters.** In his first letter, Peter feeds the lambs of Christ by showing them how to cope with the persecution that comes from outside the church; in this second letter, he teaches them to avoid the fake ministers (teachers) and wrongdoers who have come into the church.

23. **1 John: 5 chapters.** Readers of John were confronted with an early form of Gnostic teaching of Cerinthian variety. This heresy was also libertine, rejecting any moral constraint. Therefore, John wrote this letter with two fundamental goals in mind: (1) to denounce false teachers and (2) to give believers the assurance of salvation.
24. **2 John: 1 chapter.** During the first two centuries, the Gospel was preached from place to place by evangelists and itinerant teachers. Believers usually housed these missionaries in their homes and gave them food provisions for their journey when they left. Since the Gnostic teachers also used this practice, John wrote to the believers to exercise discernment in supporting the itinerant teachers.
25. **3 John: 1 chapter.** The itinerant doctors (teachers) sent by John were rejected in one of the churches of the Province of Asia by a dictatorial leader, Diotrephes. The latter even excommunicated the members who practiced hospitality towards the messengers sent by John. John wrote this letter to congratulate Gaius for having supported the doctors (teachers) indirectly warning Diotrephes.
26. **Jude: 1 chapter.** Although Jude was very eager to write to his readers concerning salvation, he felt that he should rather warn them of the presence of certain immoral men circulating among them. These were perverting the grace of God. Apparently, these false teachers were trying to convince the believers that being saved by grace gave them permission to continue to sin without fear or trembling because their sins would no longer be held against them.
27. **Revelation: 22 chapters.** John writes to encourage the faithful to firmly resist the demands of worshipping the emperor. He informs his readers that the final showdown between God and Satan is imminent. Satan will increase his persecution of believers, but

they must stand firm, even unto death. They are sealed against all spiritual evil and will soon be justified when Christ returns, when the wicked are destroyed forever, and when God's people enter into an eternity of glory and happiness.

FOREWORD #2

Simple and essential techniques for presenting a Bible study

In his book entitled *How to Prepare and Present a Bible Study* (1999), updated for Preachers, Pastors, and Laity, Dr. Enoch Saintil mentions 10 points of focus from which we choose those that are most relevant to this study, which we will reiterate here with slight adjustments:

1. To be concerned about the mandate of Matthew 28:18–20.
2. Engage in a prayer campaign for personal preparation.
3. Dedicate yourself to Bible study.
4. Dedicate yourself to diligent work for Christ.
5. Cultivate and maintain a true passion for winning souls.
6. Show kindness even in the face of threats or attacks from others.
7. Never be discouraged.

Steps to follow

Find the two people you will be studying with.

Choose the day and time of the meeting.

Customary greetings—wait until you are invited to come in and sit down. In our case (Covid-19), if the meeting is by telephone, wait for the person to answer and say they are ready to participate in the day's study. If the meeting is at your home, find a quiet place where distractions can be avoided.

Announce the topic of the day.

Say a prayer of invocation.

Begin the actual study.

Inform the Bible student of the topic for the next study.

Final prayer and separation. As soon as the study is over, without further conversation, say a prayer of blessing or, if circumstances require, a prayer of intercession and say goodbye to the Bible student. Under no circumstances agree to participate in any form of entertainment or to take food or drink.

SIMPLE AND ESSENTIAL TRUTHS #1

BY PASTOR OTHNEL PIERRE—2020

FAITH

Faith is *"pistis"* in Greek. This word is also translated as "belief". More than seventy verses have been listed in the NT speaking of Faith. Authentic Faith is important in the life of a Christian if he aspires to go to heaven.

> *Authentic Faith is important in the life of a Christian if he aspires to go to heaven.*

What is Faith?

Hebrews 11:1, "Faith is the substance of things hoped for, the evidence of things not seen."

Origin of Faith

Romans 10:17, "Faith cometh by hearing, and hearing by the word of God."

Faith bears fruit

a) Perseverance / Patience: **James 1:3**, "The trying of your faith worketh patience."

b) Vision of the glory of God: **John 11:40**, "Jesus saith unto her, 'Said I not unto thee, that, if thou wouldest believe, thou shouldest see the glory of God?'"

The only foundation of the Christian

a) Living by Faith: **2 Corinthians 5:7**, "For we walk by faith, not by sight." **Romans 1:17**, "For therein is the righteousness of God revealed from faith to faith: as it is written, The just shall live by faith."
b) Faith is key: **Hebrews. 11:6**, "Without faith it is impossible to please him: for he that cometh to God must believe that he is, and that he is a rewarder of them that diligently seek him."

Faith must be accompanied by works

a) To keep it alive: **James 2:17**, "Even so faith, if it hath not works, is dead, being alone."
b) For verification: **Mark 16:16**, "He that believeth and is baptized shall be saved; but he that believeth not shall be damned."
c) To save your soul: **Hebrews 10:38**, **39**, "Now the just shall live by faith: but if any man draw back, my soul shall have no pleasure in him. But we are not of them who draw back unto perdition; but of them that believe to the saving of the soul."

Faith makes you a child of God

John 1:12, 13, "But as many as received him, to them gave he power to become the sons of God, even to them that believe on his name: Which were born, not of blood, nor of the will of the flesh, nor of the will of man, but of God."

Faith gives you the assurance of heaven

2 Timothy 4:7, 8, "I have fought a good fight, I have finished my course, I have kept the faith: Henceforth there is laid up for me a crown of righteousness, which the Lord, the righteous judge, shall give me at that day: and not to me only, but unto all them also that love his appearing."

Questions:

1. Do you have faith in God?
2. Is it important to have faith in God?
3. What do you need to do to prove to everyone that you have faith in God?

SIMPLE AND ESSENTIAL TRUTHS #2
BY PASTOR OTHNEL PIERRE—2020

THE BIBLE

The Bible is a holy book. It is God's message in two Testaments, Old and New, for the salvation of mankind. It was written by people of different backgrounds over a period of fifteen centuries. The words are not inspired; it is the message that is inspired. The Holy Spirit ensures that the heavenly message is not altered, degraded, or defiled.

1. Pay attention to the Word

a) **Proverbs 4:20, 21**, "My son, attend to my words; incline thine ear unto my sayings. Let them not depart from thine eyes; keep them in the midst of thine heart."

b) **2 Peter 1:19–21**, "We have also a more sure word of prophecy; whereunto ye do well that ye take heed, as unto a light that shineth in a dark place, until the day dawn, and the day star arise in your hearts: Knowing this first, that no prophecy of the scripture is of any private interpretation. For the prophecy came not in old time by the will of man: but holy men of God spake as they were moved by the Holy Ghost."

2. The Word of the Lord is blameless

a. **Proverbs 30:5**, "Every word of God is pure: he is a shield unto them that put their trust in him."

b. **2 Samuel 22:31**, "As for God, his way is perfect; the word of the Lord is tried: he is a buckler to all them that trust in him."

c. **Psalm 119:160**, "Thy word is true from the beginning: and every one of thy righteous judgments endureth for ever."

d. **Psalm 19:7**, "The law of the Lord is perfect, converting the soul: the testimony of the Lord is sure, making wise the simple."

3. The Word of the Lord is everlasting

a. **Matthew 5:18**, "For verily I say unto you, Till heaven and earth pass, one jot or one tittle shall in no wise pass from the law, till all be fulfilled."

b. **1 Peter 1:23**, "Being born again, not of corruptible seed, but of incorruptible, by the word of God, which liveth and abideth for ever."

4. Benefits of the Lord's Word

a. **2 Timothy 3:16, 17**, "All scripture is given by inspiration of God, and is profitable for doctrine, for reproof, for correction, for instruction in righteousness: That the man of God may be perfect, thoroughly furnished unto all good works."
b. **John 15:7**, "If ye abide in me, and my words abide in you, ye shall ask what ye will, and it shall be done unto you."
c. **Psalm 119:11**, "Thy word have I hid in mine heart, that I might not sin against thee."
d. **John 5:39**, "Search the scriptures; for in them ye think ye have eternal life: and they are they which testify of me."

5. Obedience to the Word of the Lord is paramount

a. **Job 23:12**, "Neither have I gone back from the commandment of his lips; I have esteemed the words of his mouth more than my necessary food."
b. **Acts 2:41**, "Then they that gladly received his word were baptized: and the same day there were added unto them about three thousand souls."

Questions:

1. Does the Bible tell you what to do to have eternal life?
2. Can you become a better person simply by practicing the instructions in the Bible?
3. Is it good to know the teachings of the Bible?

SIMPLE AND ESSENTIAL TRUTHS #3

BY PASTOR OTHNEL PIERRE—2020

THE SABBATH

In the Bible, we find more than 15 verses about the day of rest or the Sabbath day. The Sabbath has a duration of 24 hours, one evening and one morning, as in Genesis 1:5. It begins on Friday at sunset and ends on Saturday at sunset. Only God's people obey God's voice. In the verses we will examine what the Lord asks His people to do on the day of worship. All those who want to be part of God's people will follow God's example.

All those who want to be part of God's people will follow God's example.

Institution of the Sabbath

a. **Genesis 2:3**, "And God blessed the seventh day, and sanctified it: because that in it he had rested from all his work which God created and made."
b. **Exodus 20:8–11**, "Remember the sabbath day, to keep it holy. Six days shalt thou labour, and do all thy work: But the seventh day is the sabbath of the Lord thy God: in it thou shalt not do any work, thou, nor thy son, nor thy daughter, thy manservant, nor thy maidservant, nor thy cattle, nor thy stranger that is within thy gates: For in six days the Lord made heaven and earth, the sea, and all that in them is, and rested the seventh day: wherefore the Lord blessed

the sabbath day, and hallowed it." (In the *Sabbath School Quarterly* "How to Interpret the Scriptures" second quarter 2020, Dr. Elias de Souza states: "The seventh-day Sabbath is under heavy attack in secularized society and in religious communities. "The Sabbath commandment is the basis for worship of the Creator. It is around this theme, worship, that the events of the last days will revolve. See Revelation 14:7).

c. **Mark 2:27, 28**, "And he said unto them, The sabbath was made for man, and not man for the sabbath: Therefore the Son of man is Lord also of the sabbath." (The Sabbath was made for man's good and happiness. The Sabbath was not for the Hebrew people alone, but for all mankind.)

The Sabbath: sign of God and man's delights

a. **Ezekiel 20:19, 20**, "I am the Lord your God; walk in my statutes, and keep my judgments, and do them; And hallow my sabbaths; and they shall be a sign between me and you, that ye may know that I am the Lord your God."

b. **Isaiah 58:13, 14**, "If thou turn away thy foot from the sabbath, from doing thy pleasure on my holy day; and call the sabbath a delight, the holy of the Lord, honourable; and shalt honour him, not doing thine own ways, nor finding thine own pleasure, nor speaking thine own words: Then shalt thou delight thyself in the Lord; and I will cause thee to ride upon the high places of the earth, and feed thee with the heritage of Jacob thy father: for the mouth of the Lord hath spoken it."

God's day of rest for His people

a. **Matthew 12:12**, "How much then is a man better than a sheep? Wherefore it is lawful to do well on the sabbath days."

b. **Leviticus 23:3**, "Six days shall work be done: but the seventh day is the sabbath of rest, an holy convocation; ye shall do no work therein: it is the sabbath of the Lord in all your dwellings."
c. There is a day of rest for God's people. Let none of you appear to have come too late. "Too late is a day before my door, and you may knock in vain." This is what **Hebrews 4:1, 9–11** says, "Let us therefore fear, lest, a promise being left us of entering into his rest, any of you should seem to come short of it. ... There remaineth therefore a rest to the people of God. For he that is entered into his rest, he also hath ceased from his own works, as God did from his. Let us labour therefore to enter into that rest, lest any man fall after the same example of unbelief."

Some of the verses spoke against the Sabbath

a. **Romans 14:5**, "One man esteemeth one day above another: another esteemeth every day alike. Let every man be fully persuaded in his own mind."
b. **Colossians 2:16–17**, "Let no man therefore judge you in meat, or in drink, or in respect of an holyday, or of the new moon, or of the sabbath days: Which are a shadow of things to come; but the body is of Christ."

The seventh-day Sabbath was here from Creation—long before the ceremonial Sabbaths.

These two verses do not speak of the seventh-day Sabbath but of the ceremonial Sabbaths. The seventh-day Sabbath was here from Creation—long before the ceremonial Sabbaths. The latter came after sin. That is why they are the shadow of things to come. Shadow is created by blocking a source of light. Before sin, there was no such blockage.

Some of the most convincing verses about the Sabbath

a. **Luke 4:16** (speaking of Jesus), "And he came to Nazareth, where he had been brought up: and, as his custom was, he went into the synagogue on the sabbath day, and stood up for to read."

b. **Matthew 28:1** (this verse allows us to identify the days: first, second, third, fourth, fifth, sixth, seventh), "In the end of the sabbath, as it began to dawn toward the first day of the week, came Mary Magdalene and the other Mary to see the sepulchre."

c. **Acts 17:1–4**, "Now when they had passed through Amphipolis and Apollonia, they came to Thessalonica, where was a synagogue of the Jews: And Paul, as his manner was, went in unto them, and three sabbath days reasoned with them out of the scriptures, Opening and alleging, that Christ must needs have suffered, and risen again from the dead; and that this Jesus, whom I preach unto you, is Christ. And some of them believed, and consorted with Paul and Silas; and of the devout Greeks a great multitude, and of the chief women not a few."

d. **Exodus 16:1–30, The Miracle of Manna**—"And they took their journey from Elim, and all the congregation of the children of Israel came unto the wilderness of Sin, which is between Elim and Sinai, on the fifteenth day of the second month after their departing out of the land of Egypt. And the whole congregation of the children of Israel murmured against Moses and Aaron in the wilderness: And the children of Israel said unto them, Would to God we had died by the hand of the Lord in the land of Egypt, when we sat by the flesh pots, and when we did eat bread to the full; for ye have brought us forth into this wilderness, to kill this whole assembly with hunger. Then said the Lord unto Moses, Behold, I will rain bread from heaven for you; and the people shall go out and gather a certain rate every day, <u>that I may prove them, whether they will walk in my law, or no</u>. And it shall come to pass, that on the sixth day they shall prepare that which they bring in; and it shall be twice as much as they gather daily. And Moses and Aaron said unto all the children of Israel, At even, then ye shall know that the Lord hath brought you out from the land of Egypt: And in the morning, then ye shall see the glory of the Lord; for that he heareth your murmurings against the Lord: and what are we, that ye murmur against us? And Moses said, This shall be, when the Lord shall give you in the evening flesh to eat, and in the morning bread to the full; for that the Lord heareth your murmurings which ye murmur against him: and what are we? your murmurings are not against us, but against the Lord. And Moses spake unto Aaron, Say unto all the congregation of the children of Israel, Come near before the Lord: for he hath heard your murmurings. And it came to pass, as Aaron spake unto the whole congregation of the children of Israel, that they looked toward the wilderness, and, behold, the glory of the Lord appeared in the cloud. And the Lord spake unto Moses, saying, I have heard the murmurings of the children of Israel: speak unto them, saying, At even ye shall eat flesh, and in the morning ye shall be filled with bread; and ye shall know that I am the Lord your God. And it came to pass, that at even the quails came up, and covered the camp: and in the morning the dew lay round about the host. And when the dew that lay was gone up, behold, upon the face of the wilderness there lay a small round thing, as small as the hoar frost on the ground. And when the children of Israel saw it, they said one to another, It is manna: for they wist not what it was. And Moses said unto them, This is the bread which the Lord hath given you to eat. This is the thing which the Lord hath commanded, Gather of it every man according to his eating, an omer for every man, according to the number of your persons; take ye every man for them which are in his tents. And the children of Israel did so, and gathered, some more, some less. And when they did mete it with an omer, he that gathered much had nothing over, and he that gathered little had no lack; they gathered every man according to his eating. And

Moses said, Let no man leave of it till the morning. Notwithstanding they hearkened not unto Moses; but some of them left of it until the morning, and it bred worms, and stank: and Moses was wroth with them. And they gathered it every morning, every man according to his eating: and when the sun waxed hot, it melted. And it came to pass, that on the sixth day they gathered twice as much bread, two omers for one man: and all the rulers of the congregation came and told Moses. And he said unto them, This is that which the Lord hath said, To morrow is the rest of the holy sabbath unto the Lord: bake that which ye will bake to day, and seethe that ye will seethe; and that which remaineth over lay up for you to be kept until the morning. And they laid it up till the morning, as Moses bade: and it did not stink, neither was there any worm therein. And Moses said, Eat that to day; for to day is a sabbath unto the Lord: to day ye shall not find it in the field. Six days ye shall gather it; but on the seventh day, which is the sabbath, in it there shall be none. And it came to pass, that there went out some of the people on the seventh day for to gather, and they found none. And the Lord said unto Moses, How long refuse ye to keep my commandments and my laws? See, for that the Lord hath given you the sabbath, therefore he giveth you on the sixth day the bread of two days; abide ye every man in his place, let no man go out of his place on the seventh day. So the people rested on the seventh day."

Questions:

1. On what day in the Bible does it say that God has bestowed a blessing?
2. Will you perish if you do not make an effort to be a Sabbath observer?
3. The Bible has given some examples of people who have observed the Sabbath; don't you want to be one of them?

SIMPLE AND ESSENTIAL TRUTHS #4

BY PASTOR OTHNEL PIERRE—2020

THE STATE OF THE DEAD

We counted more than 22 biblical verses about death in the Holy Scriptures. The subject of the fate of the dead needs special and particular attention. It is a difficult and delicate subject. It is a notion that requires the greatest amount of faith in God and His Word, due to popular beliefs that say that when someone dies, he/she goes to heaven or still participates in what is done on earth. On the other hand, because of the spiritualist phenomena—psychic reading sessions, prophecy, clairvoyance, clairaudience, gift of tongues, waving of hands, so-called "divine" healings, visions, trance, revelations, raps, levitation, and any other manifestation supporting the idea of continuity of life after death—I prefer to follow what the Bible says.

What does someone who has died know?

The Bible says in **Ecclesiastes 9:5, 6**, "For the living know that they shall die: but <u>the dead know not any thing</u>, neither have they any more a reward; for the memory of them is forgotten. Also their love, and their hatred, and their envy, is now perished; neither have they any more a portion for ever in any thing that is done under the sun."

What happens to someone who has died?

a. **Psalm 30:9**, "What profit is there in my blood, when I go down to the pit? Shall the dust praise thee? shall it declare thy truth?"
b. **Genesis 3:19**, "In the sweat of thy face shalt thou eat bread, till thou return unto the ground; for out of it wast thou taken: <u>for dust thou art, and unto dust shalt thou return</u>."
c. **Daniel 12:2**, "And <u>many of them that sleep in the dust</u> of the earth shall awake, some to everlasting life, and some to shame and everlasting contempt."
d. **John 5:28, 29**, "Marvel not at this: for the hour is coming, in the which all that are <u>in the graves</u> shall hear his voice, And shall come forth; they that have done good, unto the resurrection of life; and they that have done evil, unto the resurrection of damnation."
e. **Job 7:21**, "And why dost thou not pardon my transgression, and take away my iniquity? for now shall <u>I sleep in the dust; and thou shalt seek me in the morning, but I shall not be</u>."

The idea of someone who has died and ascended to heaven is absurd. Otherwise, 1) everyone would hurry to die; 2) we wouldn't need resurrection.

Resurrection and immortality of the righteous—Man will receive immortality at resurrection.

> a. **John 11:25, 26**, "Jesus said unto her, 'I am the resurrection, and the life: he that believeth in me, though he were dead, yet shall he live: And whosoever liveth and believeth in me shall never die. Believest thou this?'"
> b. **1 Thessalonians 4:16, 17**, "For the Lord himself shall descend from heaven with a shout, with the voice of the archangel, and with the trump of God: and the dead in Christ shall rise first: Then we which are alive and remain shall be caught up together with them in the clouds, to meet the Lord in the air: and so shall we ever be with the Lord."

Some pretextual verses: 1 Samuel 28 speaks of Saul who consulted the sorceress of En-Dor. See verse 11! "Whom shall I bring up unto thee?" —but not down.

> a. **Philippians 1:23, 24**, "For I am in a strait betwixt two, having a desire to depart, and to be with Christ; which is far better: Nevertheless to abide in the flesh is more needful for you." (Which means: to be with Christ at His next return.)
> b. **Luke 23:46**, "And when Jesus had cried with a loud voice, he said, Father, into thy hands I commend my spirit: and having said thus, he gave up the ghost." (*Ruah* in Hebrew, *pneuma* in Greek, the breath goes to God who gave it—Ecclesiastes 12:7; Genesis 2:7.)
> c. **Matthew 10:28**, "And fear not them which kill the body, but are not able to kill the soul: but rather fear him which is able to destroy both soul and body in hell." (This means that something can kill the soul—the soul is not immortal. 1 Corinthians 15:45; Genesis

2:7. The LORD God formed man from the dust of the ground. He breathed into his nostrils a breath of life and man became a living soul. Equation: dust + breath = living soul; dust - breath = dead soul.)

Source and role of Spiritualism

a. **Genesis 3:4**, "And the serpent said unto the woman, Ye shall not surely die." (This is the basis of Spiritualism. On this basis, the dead are more alive in their dead state than when they were alive.)
b. **Matthew 24:24, 25**, "For there shall arise false Christs, and false prophets, and shall shew great signs and wonders; insomuch that, if it were possible, they shall deceive the very elect. Behold, I have told you before." (False Christs will use spiritualism.)
c. **1 Timothy 4:1**, "Now the Spirit speaketh expressly, that in the latter times some shall depart from the faith, giving heed to seducing spirits, and doctrines of devils." (Many will be deceived).
d. **Revelation 16:14**, "For they are the spirits of devils, working miracles, which go forth unto the kings of the earth and of the whole world, to gather them to the battle of that great day of God Almighty."
e. **1 Corinthians 10:20**, "But I say, that the things which the Gentiles sacrifice, they sacrifice to devils, and not to God: and I would not that ye should have fellowship with devils."
f. **Galatians 5:19–21**, "Now the works of the flesh are manifest, which are these; Adultery, fornication, uncleanness, lasciviousness, Idolatry, witchcraft, hatred, variance, emulations, wrath, strife, seditions, heresies, Envyings, murders, drunkenness, revellings, and such like: of the which I tell you before, as I have also told you in time past, that they which do such things shall not inherit the kingdom of God."

Questions:

1. Do you prefer to listen to popular beliefs or to the Bible?
2. Do Satan and his disguised followers always tell lies?
3. What do you think will happen to people who continue to believe that the dead are still part of their daily activities?
4. What do you want to do now that you know the truth about the State of the Dead? I want to pray for you.

SIMPLE AND ESSENTIAL TRUTHS #5

BY PASTOR OTHNEL PIERRE—2020

HEALTH PRINCIPLES

Our body being the temple of the Holy Spirit, we must take proper care of it. In addition to adequate exercise and rest, we must adopt the healthiest possible diet and abstain from unhealthy foods mentioned as such in Scripture. Alcoholic beverages, tobacco, and the use of drugs and narcotics are harmful to our bodies, so we must also abstain from them. Instead, we will use anything that will subject our bodies and thoughts to the authority of Christ, who desires us to be healthy, happy, and fulfilled.

God cares for the sick

a. **Matthew 9:12**, "But when Jesus heard that, he said unto them, They that be whole need not a physician, but they that are sick."
b. **Matthew 10:8**, "Heal the sick, cleanse the lepers, raise the dead, cast out devils: freely ye have received, freely give." (This is what Jesus asked his disciples to do.)
c. **Psalms 147:3**, "He healeth the broken in heart, and bindeth up their wounds." (This is Heaven's greatest concern.)
d. **Exodus 23:25**, "And ye shall serve the Lord your God, and he shall bless thy bread, and thy water; and I will take sickness away from the midst of thee." (He must be served.)

Additional Health Tips

a. **Ecclesiastes 11:10**, "Therefore remove sorrow from thy heart, and put away evil from thy flesh: for childhood and youth are vanity."
b. **Matthew 6:27**, "Which of you by taking thought can add one cubit unto his stature?" (Avoid them.)
c. **1 Timothy 4:8**, "For bodily exercise profiteth little: but godliness is profitable unto all things, having promise of the life that now is, and of that which is to come." (Practice.)
d. **Proverbs 17:22**, "A merry heart doeth good like a medicine: but a broken spirit drieth the bones." (Whatever happens, always smile.)

Children of God are called to sanctification (To fight and avoid disease).

a. **Daniel 1:8**, "But Daniel purposed in his heart that he would not defile himself with the portion of the king's meat, nor with the

wine which he drank: therefore he requested of the prince of the eunuchs that he might not defile himself."
   b. **Romans 12:1**, "I beseech you therefore, brethren, by the mercies of God, that ye present your bodies a living sacrifice, holy, acceptable unto God, which is your reasonable service."
   c. **Colossians 2:21**, "Touch not; taste not; handle not."
   d. **1 Peter 2:9**, "But ye are a chosen generation, a royal priesthood, an holy nation, a peculiar people; that ye should shew forth the praises of him who hath called you out of darkness into his marvellous light."

Sanctification of body and spirit (If you know that someone is doing something unpleasant in the Lord...).

   a. **2 Corinthians 6:17, 18**, "Wherefore come out from among them, and be ye separate, saith the Lord, and touch not the unclean thing; and I will receive you. And will be a Father unto you, and ye shall be my sons and daughters, saith the Lord Almighty." (See also Psalm 27:10.)
   b. **3 John 1:2**, "Beloved, I wish above all things that thou mayest prosper and be in health, even as thy soul prospereth."

Eating and drinking is part of religion

   a. **1 Corinthians 10:31**, "Whether therefore ye eat, or drink, or whatsoever ye do, do all to the glory of God."
   b. **Leviticus 11 and Deuteronomy 14** tell us what animals, birds, and fish to eat:

Among the animals that live on earth, if we consider reptiles to be negligible, those that are acceptable (edible) are those that fulfill these three conditions: the split horn, the forked foot, and the ruminants. Among the animals that are in the water, they must meet two conditions:

fins and scales. Among the birds, climbers (woodpeckers, parrots), birds of prey (hawks, eagles), nocturnal birds (owls), and those with webbed feet (ducks, geese) should be avoided.

Practice the original diet (as much as possible)

Genesis 1:29, "And God said, Behold, I have given you every <u>herb bearing seed</u>, which is upon the face of all the earth, and <u>every tree, in the which is the fruit of a tree yielding seed</u>; to you it shall be for meat."

Triumph over intemperance

1 Corinthians 9:25, "And every man that striveth for the <u>mastery</u> is temperate in all things. Now they do it to obtain a corruptible crown; but we an incorruptible."

<u>**Alcoholic beverages**</u> (Besides meat as food, God also speaks of drink, stimulants, and narcotics).

a. **Proverbs 20:1**, "Wine is a mocker, strong drink is raging: and whosoever is deceived thereby is not wise."
b. **Proverbs 23:29–33**, "Who hath woe? who hath sorrow? who hath contentions? who hath babbling? who hath wounds without cause? who hath redness of eyes? They that tarry long at the wine; they that go to seek mixed wine. Look not thou upon the wine when it is red, when it giveth his colour in the cup, when it moveth itself aright. At the last it biteth like a serpent, and stingeth like an adder. Thine eyes shall behold strange women, and thine heart shall utter perverse things."
c. **Leviticus 10:9, 10**, "Do not drink wine nor strong drink, thou, nor thy sons with thee, when ye go into the tabernacle of the congregation, lest ye die: it shall be a statute for ever throughout your generations: And that ye may put difference between holy and unholy, and between unclean and clean."
d. **Ephesians 5:18**, "And be not drunk with wine, wherein is excess; but be filled with the Spirit."

e. **1 Timothy 3:3**, "Not given to wine, no striker, not greedy of filthy lucre; but patient, not a brawler, not covetous."
f. **1 Corinthians 5:11**, "It is forbidden even to eat with a person who calls himself a Christian and is drunk. But now I have written unto you not to keep company, if any man that is called a brother be a fornicator, or covetous, or an idolator, or a railer, or a drunkard, or an extortioner; with such an one no not to eat."

Stimulants and narcotics (Tobacco, Caffeine, and Drugs) **Deuteronomy 29:18**, "Lest there should be among you man, or woman, or family, or tribe, whose heart turneth away this day from the Lord our God, to go and serve the gods of these nations; lest there should be among you a root that beareth gall and wormwood."

Significance of Peter's vision (Some people take the vision of Peter's tablecloth as an excuse to eat anything. Following is the correct meaning.)

Acts 10:28, 34, 35, "And he said unto them, Ye know how that it is an unlawful thing for a man that is a Jew to keep company, or come unto one of another nation; but God hath shewed me that I should not call any man common or unclean. Then Peter opened his mouth, and said, Of a truth I perceive that God is no respecter of persons: But in every nation he that feareth him, and worketh righteousness, is accepted with him."

Other pretextual verses

a. **Matthew 15:11**, "Not that which goeth into the mouth defileth a man; but that which cometh out of the mouth, this defileth a man." (Follow the context: to make the washing of hands a ritual of eternal salvation.)
b. **1 Corinthians 10:25–31**, "Whatsoever is sold in the shambles, that eat, asking no question for conscience sake: For the earth is the Lord's, and the fulness thereof. If any of them that believe not bid you to a feast, and ye be disposed to go; whatsoever is set before you, eat, asking no question for conscience sake. But if any man

say unto you, this is offered in sacrifice unto idols, eat not for his sake that shewed it, and for conscience sake: for the earth is the Lord's, and the fulness thereof: Conscience, I say, not thine own, but of the other: for why is my liberty judged of another man's conscience? For if I by grace be a partaker, why am I evil spoken of for that for which I give thanks? Whether therefore ye eat, or drink, or whatsoever ye do, do all to the glory of God."

c. **Romans 14:14–17**, "I know, and am persuaded by the Lord Jesus, that there is nothing unclean of itself: but to him that esteemeth any thing to be unclean, to him it is unclean. But if thy brother be grieved with thy meat, now walkest thou not charitably. Destroy not him with thy meat, for whom Christ died. Let not then your good be evil spoken of: For the kingdom of God is not meat and drink; but righteousness, and peace, and joy in the Holy Ghost."

d. **1 Timothy 4:4, 5**, "For every creature of God is good, and nothing to be refused, if it be received with thanksgiving: For it is sanctified by the word of God and prayer."

e. **Titus 1:15**, "Unto the pure all things are pure: but unto them that are defiled and unbelieving is nothing pure; but even their mind and conscience is defiled."

(The verses indicated here in b, c, d, e, have no connection with the pure and unclean foods of Leviticus 11 and Deuteronomy 14. The explanation of all this is given in 1 Corinthians 8:7–13.)

What is the rationale behind all of these verses by Paul?

a. **1 Corinthians 8:7–13**, "Howbeit there is not in every man that knowledge: for some with conscience of the idol unto this hour eat it as a thing offered unto an idol; and their conscience being weak is defiled. But meat commendeth us not to God: for neither, if we eat, are we the better; neither, if we eat not, are we the worse.

But take heed lest by any means this liberty of yours become a stumblingblock to them that are weak. For if any man see thee which hast knowledge sit at meat in the idol's temple, shall not the conscience of him which is weak be emboldened to eat those things which are offered to idols; And through thy knowledge shall the weak brother perish, for whom Christ died? But when ye sin so against the brethren, and wound their weak conscience, ye sin against Christ. Wherefore, if meat make my brother to offend, I will eat no flesh while the world standeth, lest I make my brother to offend."

b. **2 Peter 3:16, 17** (Apostle Peter identifies those who have difficulty understanding this simple and essential truth and encourages those who understand it to hold fast), "As also in all his epistles, speaking in them of these things; in which are some things hard to be understood, which they that are unlearned and unstable wrest, as they do also the other scriptures, unto their own destruction. Ye therefore, beloved, seeing ye know these things before, beware lest ye also, being led away with the error of the wicked, fall from your own stedfastness."

Consequences (If you persist in disobeying divine injunctions, you will pay the consequences).

If you persist in disobeying divine injunctions, you will pay the consequences.

Isaiah 66:17, "They that sanctify themselves, and purify themselves in the gardens behind one tree in the midst, eating swine's flesh, and the abomination, and the mouse, shall be consumed together, saith the Lord."

National Geographic Magazine, November 2005, speaks of the Adventist people in these terms: Through the Bible (the human body is the temple of God—1 Corinthians 6:19), the Adventist Church advocates health reform including a healthy diet, maintenance of the body through physical exercise, abstinence from alcohol, tobacco and other harmful substances.

Several studies indicate that the life expectancy of Adventists is higher than the average for the population of developed countries (4 years longer for women and 7 years longer for men).

Blessing on him who obeys—And if you obey God's injunctions, this is the blessing that will come with you.)

1 Thessalonians 5:23, "And the very God of peace sanctify you wholly; and I pray God your whole spirit and soul and body be preserved blameless unto the coming of our Lord Jesus Christ."

Questions:

1. Do you want to be among those who choose to obey?
2. Those who eat pig flesh will perish; what would you have preferred? Perish or give up eating pork and abominable things?
3. God cares about you in every way. Do you want to tell God that you belong to Him now and forever?

SIMPLE AND ESSENTIAL TRUTHS #6

PREPARED BY PASTOR OTHNEL PIERRE—2020

THE LORD'S SUPPER

Who can participate in the Lord's Supper?

The following study is important because it deals with a topic that concerns a practical element of our faith. As with my other suggestions for information, I present this theme in a very simple way. The Lord's Supper symbolizes our acceptance of the body and blood of Jesus, shed and broken for us. Probing our hearts, we wash each other's feet, remembering Jesus' example of humility and service. The Lord's Supper (or "supper" etymologically, "breaking of bread," "Lord's supper," "Lord's table") is the participation in the emblems of the body and blood of Jesus; it expresses our faith in him, our Lord and Savior. In this experience of communion, Christ is present to meet his people and strengthen them. By joyfully taking part in it, we proclaim the Lord's death until He comes. Preparation for the service of communion involves an examination of conscience, repentance, and confession. The Master prescribed the washing of the feet to symbolize a renewed purification, to express a readiness to serve one another in Christ-like humility, and to unite our hearts in love. The service of communion is open to all Christians.

> *The Lord's Supper symbolizes our acceptance of the body and blood of Jesus, shed and broken for us.*

Institution of the Holy Communion

John 13:1–17, "Now before the feast of the passover, when Jesus knew that his hour was come that he should depart out of this world unto the Father, having loved his own which were in the world, he loved them unto the end. And supper being ended, the devil having now put into the heart of Judas Iscariot, Simon's son, to betray him; Jesus knowing that the Father had given all things into his hands, and that he was come from God, and went to God; He riseth from supper, and laid aside his garments; and took a towel, and girded himself. After that he poureth water into a bason, and began to wash the disciples' feet, and to wipe them with the towel wherewith he was girded. Then cometh he to Simon Peter: and Peter saith unto him, Lord, dost thou wash my feet? Jesus answered and said unto him, What I do thou knowest not now; but thou shalt know hereafter. Peter saith unto him, Thou shalt never wash my feet. Jesus answered him, If I wash thee not, thou hast no part with me. Simon Peter saith unto him, Lord, not my feet only, but also my hands and my head. Jesus saith to him, He that is washed needeth not save to wash his feet, but is clean every whit: and ye are clean, but not all. For he knew who should betray him; therefore said he, Ye are not all clean.

"So after he had washed their feet, and had taken his garments, and was set down again, he said unto them, Know ye what I have done to you? Ye call me Master and Lord: and ye say well; for so I am. If I then, your Lord and Master, have washed your feet; ye also ought to wash one another's feet. For I have given you an example, that ye should do as I have done to you. Verily, verily, I say unto you, The servant is not greater than his lord; neither he that is sent greater than he that sent him. If ye know these things, happy are ye if ye do them."

Three things are important in a correct Lord's Supper: 1) The washing of the feet, which is a service of humility; 2) Unleavened bread; 3) The pure juice of the vine.

Matthew 26:26–30, "And as they were eating, Jesus took bread, and blessed it, and brake it, and gave it to the disciples, and said, Take, eat; this is my body. And he took the cup, and gave thanks, and gave it to them, saying, Drink ye all of it; For this is my blood of the new testament, which is shed for many for the remission of sins. But I say unto you, I will not drink henceforth of this fruit of the vine, until that day when I drink it new with you in my Father's kingdom. And when they had sung an hymn, they went out into the mount of Olives."

Jesus is very careful in the example he gives us in instituting the Lord's Supper: 1) He took the bread, gave thanks, that is, blessed the bread, broke it, that is, broke it into pieces and gave a token to each disciple. 2) He took the cup, gave thanks, that is, blessed the juice of the vine and distributed it to the disciples.

1 Corinthians 11:20–34, "When ye come together therefore into one place, this is not to eat the Lord's supper. For in eating every one taketh before other his own supper: and one is hungry, and another is drunken. What? have ye not houses to eat and to drink in? or despise ye the church of God, and shame them that have not? what shall I say to you? shall I praise you in this? I praise you not. For I have received of the Lord that which also I delivered unto you, that the Lord Jesus the same night in which he was betrayed took bread: And when he had given thanks, he brake it, and said, Take, eat: this is my body, which is broken for you: this do in remembrance of me. After the same manner also he took the cup, when he had supped, saying, this cup is the new testament in my blood: this do ye, as oft as ye drink it, in remembrance of me. For as often as ye eat this bread, and drink this cup, ye do shew the Lord's death till he come. Wherefore whosoever shall eat this bread, and drink this cup of the Lord, unworthily, shall be guilty of the body and blood of the Lord. But let a man examine himself, and so let him eat of that bread, and drink of that cup. For he that eateth and drinketh unworthily, eateth and drinketh damnation to himself, not discerning the Lord's body. For this cause many are weak and sickly among you, and many sleep. For if we would judge ourselves, we should not be judged. But when we are judged, we are chastened of the Lord, that we should not be condemned with the world. Wherefore, my brethren, when ye come together to eat, tarry one for another. And if any man hunger, let him eat at home; that ye come not together unto condemnation. And the rest will I set in order when I come."

Paul's account (about A.D. 51) is the oldest document we have on the Lord's Supper. In organizing the Church of Corinth, the apostle had prescribed the celebration of this memorial meal.

When to take the Lord's Supper?

Jesus did not specify when and at what intervals the disciples would have to take the Lord's Supper. The commandment, "Do this in memory of me whenever you drink it" (1 Corinthians 11:25), however, seems to indicate a frequent celebration. The Seventh-day Adventist Church has prescribed quarterly frequency. The most important element of the Lord's Supper is communion.

Who can participate in the Holy Communion, at the Lord's Supper, at the Lord's table?

1. Those who believe in Him, for the forgiveness of their sin and their eternal redemption: **Romans 5:8**, "But God commendeth his love toward us, in that, while we were yet sinners, Christ died for us." Christ died for me.
2. Those who belong to the Lord, who are conscious of being redeemed by His blood to be His.
   - **1 Corinthians 7:23**, "Ye are bought with a price; be not ye the servants of men."
   - **Hebrews 9:12**, "Neither by the blood of goats and calves, but by his own blood he entered in once into the holy place, having obtained eternal redemption for us."
3. His disciples, those who have received His Word and have been baptized, keep His teachings and practice His instructions. **Matthew 28:19, 20**, "Go ye therefore, and teach all nations, baptizing them in the name of the Father, and of the Son, and of the Holy Ghost: Teaching them to observe all things whatsoever I have commanded you: and, lo, I am with you always, even unto the end of the world. Amen."
4. His faithful who have made a covenant with Him through sacrifice, who remain attached to Him and follow Him. **Psalm 50:5**, "Gather my saints together unto me; those that have made a covenant with me by sacrifice."

<u>Additional advice:</u>
- Do not deprive yourself of the blessing of the Lord's Supper. **1 Corinthians 11:26**, "For as often as ye eat this bread, and drink this cup, ye do shew the Lord's death till he come."
- There is one element on which we should be most vigilant: that of the morality of the members of the body of Christ who participate in the Lord's Supper. **Hebrews 10:24**, "And let us consider one another to provoke unto love and to good works."

- Now, if we eat the Lord's Supper with people who call themselves brothers and sisters, who live ostensibly in sin, that we know it and keep silent, we make ourselves accomplices in their situation. **1 Corinthians 5:11**, "But now I have written unto you not to keep company, if any man that is called a brother be a fornicator, or covetous, or an idolator, or a railer, or a drunkard, or an extortioner; with such an one no not to eat."
- We must not trivialize the Lord's Supper, but take it respectfully in faith, with gratitude and thanksgiving, with attentive listening to the Holy Spirit of God who often speaks at that time. **John 14:25, 26**, "These things have I spoken unto you, being yet present with you. But the Comforter, which is the Holy Ghost, whom the Father will send in my name, he shall teach you all things, and bring all things to your remembrance, whatsoever I have said unto you."

Questions:

1. Who instituted the Lord's Supper—Jesus or the Apostles?
2. Is it important to see all three elements—foot washing, unleavened bread, pure juice from the vine—in a Lord's Supper ceremony?
3. What makes this service solemn in addition to the presence of Jesus?

SIMPLE AND ESSENTIAL TRUTHS #7

PREPARED BY PASTOR OTHNEL PIERRE—2020

FIDELITY EXERCISES

You have surely heard about this Belgian Italian singer, Salvatore, Knight Adamo (born November 1, 1943). Google and YouTube can help you learn more about him. He is a singer-songwriter, best known for his romantic ballads. One of his songs said: "Miss, wait! You're carrying my heart in your purse. And if you keep it, you will make its happiness and even more mine. "Since the fall, the heart of humanity is in the Devil's handbag. The only proof that we can have that it has been cleared by Christ is your willingness to give selflessly, faithfully, joyfully, eagerly, and without murmuring for the Lord's cause. This can only be possible through the more than Herculean strength of your love for Jesus, through faith. Giving for the Lord's cause translates into giving 100% of one's being, i.e. one's body, time, talents, and money. Your heart is in the Devil's handbag. And if he keeps it, he will do it hurt and yours even more. The Lord wants to redeem it today. He will make it happy, and He will make you happy even more. The visible sign that these four notions are found in someone, starts from the value he/she places on his/her income and possessions.

Measurement of a man

- **Matthew 6:19–21**, Lay not up for yourselves treasures upon earth, where moth and rust doth corrupt, and where thieves break through and steal: But lay up for yourselves treasures in heaven, where neither moth nor rust doth corrupt, and where thieves do not break through nor steal: (A man is measured by the yardstick of his heart.)
- **Proverbs 22:7**, "The rich ruleth over the poor, and the borrower is servant to the lender." (Your will to share determines the state of your heart.)
- **The episode of the rich young man:** Matthew 19:16–26, "And, behold, one came and said unto him, Good Master, what good thing shall I do, that I may have eternal life? And he said unto him, Why callest thou me good? there is none good but one, that is, God: but if thou wilt enter into life, keep the commandments. He saith unto him, Which? Jesus said, Thou shalt do no murder, Thou shalt not commit adultery, Thou shalt not steal, Thou shalt not bear false witness, Honour thy father and thy mother: and, Thou shalt love thy neighbour as thyself. The young man saith

unto him, All these things have I kept from my youth up: what lack I yet? Jesus said unto him, If thou wilt be perfect, go and sell that thou hast, and give to the poor, and thou shalt have treasure in heaven: and come and follow me. But when the young man heard that saying, he went away sorrowful: for he had great possessions. Then said Jesus unto his disciples, Verily I say unto you, That a rich man shall hardly enter into the kingdom of heaven. And again I say unto you, It is easier for a camel to go through the eye of a needle, than for a rich man to enter into the kingdom of God. When his disciples heard it, they were exceedingly amazed, saying, Who then can be saved? But Jesus beheld them, and said unto them, With men this is impossible; but with God all things are possible."

- **1 Chronicles 29:17**, "I know also, my God, that thou triest the heart, and hast pleasure in uprightness. As for me, in the uprightness of mine heart I have willingly offered all these things: and now have I seen with joy thy people, which are present here, to offer willingly unto thee."

Proof of your love for God

- **Proverbs 3:9, 10**, "Honour the Lord with thy substance, and with the firstfruits of all thine increase: So shall thy barns be filled with plenty, and thy presses shall burst out with new wine."
- **1 Chronicles 29:13, 14**, "Now therefore, our God, we thank thee, and praise thy glorious name. But who am I, and what is my people, that we should be able to offer so willingly after this sort? for all things come of thee, and of thine own have we given thee."
- **Perpetual vow to the LORD. Genesis 28:22**, "And this stone, which I have set for a pillar, shall be God's house: and of all that thou shalt give me I will surely give the tenth unto thee."

This is a command though

- **Exodus 35:5, 22, 26, 29**, "Take ye from among you an offering unto the Lord: whosoever is of a willing heart, let him bring it, an offering of the Lord; gold, and silver, and brass, And they came, both men and women, as many as were willing hearted, and brought bracelets, and earrings, and rings, and tablets, all jewels of gold: and every man that offered offered an offering of gold unto the Lord. And all the women whose heart stirred them up in wisdom spun goats' hair."
- **2 Corinthians 9:7**, "Every man according as he purposeth in his heart, so let him give; not grudgingly, or of necessity: for God loveth a cheerful giver."
- **1 Corinthians 4:2**, "Moreover it is required in stewards, that a man be found faithful."
- **Matthew 23:23**, "Woe unto you, scribes and Pharisees, hypocrites! for ye pay tithe of mint and anise and cummin, and have omitted the weightier matters of the law, judgment, mercy, and faith: these ought ye to have done, and not to leave the other undone."

<u>Obedience</u>. Exodus 35:20, 21, "And all the congregation of the children of Israel departed from the presence of Moses. And they came, every one whose heart stirred him up, and every one whom his spirit made willing, and they brought the Lord's offering to the work of the tabernacle of the congregation, and for all his service, and for the holy garments."

Blessings that will follow

- **Proverbs 11:25**, "The liberal soul shall be made fat: and he that watereth shall be watered also himself."
- **Malachi 3:7–12**, "Even from the days of your fathers ye are gone away from mine ordinances, and have not kept them. Return unto

me, and I will return unto you, saith the Lord of hosts. But ye said, Wherein shall we return? Will a man rob God? Yet ye have robbed me. But ye say, Wherein have we robbed thee? In tithes and offerings. Ye are cursed with a curse: for ye have robbed me, even this whole nation. Bring ye all the tithes into the storehouse, that there may be meat in mine house, and prove me now herewith, saith the Lord of hosts, if I will not open you the windows of heaven, and pour you out a blessing, that there shall not be room enough to receive it. And I will rebuke the devourer for your sakes, and he shall not destroy the fruits of your ground; neither shall your vine cast her fruit before the time in the field, saith the Lord of hosts. And all nations shall call you blessed: for ye shall be a delightsome land, saith the Lord of hosts."

Woe to him that deceives God

- **Acts 5:9**, "Then Peter said unto her, How is it that ye have agreed together to tempt the Spirit of the Lord? behold, the feet of them which have buried thy husband are at the door, and shall carry thee out."
- **Luke 12: 20, 21**, "But God said unto him, Thou fool, this night thy soul shall be required of thee: then whose shall those things be, which thou hast provided? So is he that layeth up treasure for himself, and is not rich toward God."
- **Deuteronomy 8:17–19**, "And thou say in thine heart, My power and the might of mine hand hath gotten me this wealth. But thou shalt remember the Lord thy God: for it is he that giveth thee power to get wealth, that he may establish his covenant which he sware unto thy fathers, as it is this day. And it shall be, if thou do at all forget the Lord thy God, and walk after other gods, and serve them, and worship them, I testify against you this day that ye shall surely perish."

Additional salutary advice

- **Leviticus 27:30, 31**, "And all the tithe of the land, whether of the seed of the land, or of the fruit of the tree, is the Lord's: it is holy unto the Lord. And if a man will at all redeem ought of his tithes, he shall add thereto the fifth part thereof." [Do not lend or borrow anything that has been set apart for the Lord. In case this happens, add to it ($200.00 : 5 = $40.00 => $240.00)].
- **Luke 12:15**, "And he said unto them, Take heed, and beware of covetousness: for a man's life consisteth not in the abundance of the things which he possesseth."
- **Acts 20:35**, "I have shewed you all things, how that so labouring ye ought to support the weak, and to remember the words of the Lord Jesus, how he said, It is more blessed to give than to receive."
- Bring tithes and offerings. "Tithes" means 10% of your income and offerings will be given according to the measure of your love and faith in God. Some give the same amount as tithe; others give half the value of tithe; and still others give more than the value of tithe as offerings. (Examples may be given to or by the Student, if appropriate.)

Questions:

1. Why do we have to return tithes and offerings to God?
2. What promise does God make to the one who faithfully returns tithes and offerings?
3. What perpetual vow do you want to make to the LORD?

IN CONCLUSION...

In **John 10:16**, Jesus says, "And other sheep I have, which are not of this fold: them also I must bring, and they shall hear my voice; and there shall be one fold, and one shepherd."

This compendium can help in this regard. It can be used as an instrument for personal evangelization or for a week of public evangelization. In it we have brought together the best of the key topics of the Adventist Movement for the satisfaction of all, pastors and dedicated lay people. The reader or listener who adheres to these principles will be a nail planted and sealed in the Church by Christ himself. And he or she will be like the house built on the rock of **Matthew 7:24, 25**, "Therefore whosoever heareth these sayings of mine, and doeth them, I will liken him unto a wise man, which built his house upon a rock: And the rain descended, and the floods came, and the winds blew, and beat upon that house; and it fell not: for it was founded upon a rock." May God by His Holy Spirit allow you to make good use of it, so that the other sheep may be brought to the pasture and there may be one flock and one Shepherd. I can't wait to come home. How about you?

REVIEWS

"This little manual is a practical tool that demonstrates the importance of individual involvement in evangelism. Above all, it aims to facilitate the task of every Christian in his divine mission to serve the Master. With this collection you can be confident in utilizing the basic essentials of evangelism. This goes beyond the star preacher at public evangelism campaigns and the few helpers seen up front ... you no longer have to be only a spectator. Thus, the **Glwa Pou Bondye Team** joins me in first congratulating Pastor Othnel Pierre for this initiative and for encouraging you to make use of this new resource."

—*Dorcéna Dorzilmé, MPA, B.Ed.*
Author, trainer, coach, speaker
President of the Glwa Pou Bondye Team

"According to the Bible, one of the most important roles of the pastor is to work for "the perfecting of the saints for the work of ministry and for the building up of the body of Christ." By producing this concise work, Pastor Othnel Pierre responds to the biblical imperative. It also empowers lay members to take an active role in spreading the gospel by ministering to all believers. For too long the church has drifted into the mistaken position that undertaking Bible studies and conducting evangelism is the sole responsibility of the pastor. This booklet serves as a tool to reset the role of each member of the church in evangelism outreach."

—Daniel Honoré
President of the Northeastern Conference
of Seventh-day Adventists

"MAKING DISCIPLES FOR CHRIST IN SEVEN DAYS is not an express program of evangelism, nor is it the end of mass evangelistic campaigns. This is the catalog of a disciple's life preparing to meet the Lord Jesus. It is a program that educates and strengthens. It is also a guide to «returning to the old paths,» to a life of service for the Master in a postmodern world—a postmodern world which does not deny religion but empties it of its essence."

—Jean Josué Pierre
Dean of the Faculty of Educational Sciences,
Adventist University of Haiti

"The evidence of nature makes it inexcusable to eliminate God from its testimony. In His love, God uses, in addition to the cosmos, humans, created in His image, to proclaim his Commandments. Human disobedience and estrangement from God, however, do not dissuade the Most High from maintaining His relationship with His creation. God's plan for renewal and happiness, coupled with redemption, are the excellent gifts which the Lord gives to His children. During this time of pandemic, Pastor Othnel Pierre utilizes the publication method to work tirelessly in search of souls thirsty for the water of life that only Jesus Christ gives. This collection, MAKING DISCIPLES FOR CHRIST IN SEVEN DAYS, represents an easy guide leading any reader to the source of this water of life."

—Aléus Alcin
Elder, Mitspa SDA Church

"If the completion of the proclamation of the gospel requires the combined effort of pastors and laity, any real step towards equipping them for the accomplishment of this task is of the utmost importance and of the most pressing demand. Here then is the vision which impassioned the spirit of Pastor Othnel Pierre and which generated in him the great desire to equip our members by making available to them this work, MAKING DISCIPLES FOR CHRIST IN SEVEN DAYS, a seemingly simple tool, but yet powerful enough to better train the army of the Lord to overthrow the strongholds of the formidable adversary by submitting them to King Jesus. We praise the author's initiative and say: Glory to God!"

—*Pasteur Yrvain Jean-Philippe*
Ph.D.

We invite you to view the complete
selection of titles we publish at:
www.TEACHServices.com

We encourage you to write us
with your thoughts about this,
or any other book we publish at:
info@TEACHServices.com

TEACH Services' titles may be purchased in
bulk quantities for educational, fund-raising,
business, or promotional use.
bulksales@TEACHServices.com

Finally, if you are interested in seeing
your own book in print, please contact us at:
publishing@TEACHServices.com
We are happy to review your manuscript at no charge.

www.ingramcontent.com/pod-product-compliance
Lightning Source LLC
Chambersburg PA
CBHW070546170426
43200CB00011B/2570